A CROWN OF BEAUTY INSTEAD OF ASHES

A Woman Who Overcame the Silence
of Abuse, Neglect, and Rejection

GRACE SHALON

WESTBOW
PRESS®
A DIVISION OF THOMAS NELSON
& ZONDERVAN

WestBow Press books may be ordered through booksellers or by contacting:

WestBow Press
A Division of Thomas Nelson & Zondervan
1663 Liberty Drive
Bloomington, IN 47403
www.westbowpress.com
844-714-3454

Scripture is from the King James Version of the Bible.

ISBN: 978-1-6642-2391-2 (sc)
ISBN: 978-1-6642-2392-9 (e)

Library of Congress Control Number: 2021903217

Print information available on the last page.

WestBow Press rev. date: 6/2/2021

TESTIMONIALS

Grace Shalon is very passionate about prayer and seeing God move through the power of intercessory prayer. She's a great mom who loves her children no matter what we do. I am very grateful to have her as my mom.

—My son Emmanuel

Grace Shalon will show you how God can take the foolish things of this world to confound the wise. In her story you will see that she never gave up on her hopes and dreams. It is never too late. As long as one has breath in his or her body, we can accomplish anything with Christ.

—Family friend

Grace Shalon gives details on how praying and believing God will change the course of one's life from negative to positive.

—My Mother Cindy

To God, the Lord Most High, who kept His hands on my life. When others gave up and counted me for dead, You were there. Thank You for placing greatness and purpose inside me. You deserve all glory and honor.

Mom, you never gave up. You continued to encourage me even when I wanted to give up and walk away. Thank you for always believing in me.

To my three children, I look at each of you and say, "I want better for you." You all push me further than my flesh would like to go. Mommy loves you.

SPECIAL THANKS

Thank you to all those who labored in the faith with me and helped me along the way. I cannot express my gratitude to all my friends and family who believed in me, encouraged me through this process, or offered a shoulder to cry on. It's been a journey.

Thank you for those ministers who walked with me while I endured my major deliverance. It was worth it.

Thank you to my two beautiful sisters in Christ, who helped me in the editing process. I could not have done it without you.

To my pastors who believed in me and prayed for my family and me and who continue to encourage and challenge me to reach my full potential. Thank you.

Thank You, God, for allowing me to share this story that it may bring healing, deliverance, and hope to someone else. I'm very thankful to God for the opportunity to live this dream out in my life. I would not change my life, as this is my portion that the Lord has given me. Thank You, Lord, for, "surrounding those that surround me." You are for me.

FROM THE HEART

I desire to remind those of you who have had lives full of obstacles that you can make it. Never give up on yourself. Know that you are not alone. The Father is always there, but one must first run to Him. He will save and deliver you from every yoke of bondage or curse that may have been spoken over you. Ask God to give you the desire to want to live for Him and follow Him all the days of your life. I'm not telling you every day will be easy, but there is a peace that only comes from having a relationship with God. Everything I needed was found in Him. After all the years of trying to fill the voids in my life, I concluded that Jesus is the answer. I went from a third-grade education and having special needs and comprehension issues to earning a college degree. Once

I learned how to get in God's Word and applied it to my life, I was changed forever.

If you think you don't have anyone, remember you have God fighting for your sanity, mind, freedom, family, and life. If you decide to follow Christ, I promise you will not regret it. This was the best thing that could ever happen to me. If you don't know Christ and would like to experience a new life, repeat after me:

> Lord, I am a sinner standing in need of forgiveness of my sins. Come into my heart and come into my mind. I believe that You died on the cross for me and rose from the dead (1 Corinthians 15:4). I walk away from the life of sin and allow you to have full access to my life. Come into my heart Lord, and save me and change my life.

If you said this prayer, I'm excited to say you are now saved. Enjoy your new journey, and remember you are no longer a slave to sin.

PURPOSE FOR SHARING MY STORY

1. Let others know what the enemy intended for evil, God will turn around for your good.

2. Silence the enemy concerning my life's destination.

3. Take back what the enemy stole.

4. Show others that when you have been thrown away and rejected, God yet accepts you.

5. To encourage others to follow their hearts. Die empty, allowing your dreams to live.

6. Finally, yet most important, prove to myself that I can do all things through Christ, who gives me strength.

One

COME TAKE A LOOK

My name is Grace Shalon. I was born January 9, 1972, to Cindy and Matthew, in a little town in New Jersey. I grew up in a home with two working parents who wanted to give me the best of life. When

I was a little girl, Dad would take Mom and me to the beach, and we would play and enjoy life. Mom and Dad were very creative. They designed my clothing, making sure I always looked nice; after all, I was a reflection of them both. My parents were very classy. Their appearance meant a lot to them.

Mom was very passive, and Dad was very domineering and boisterous. When he spoke, you listened. Because of the way he spoke, he was sure to get his point across. I recall like it was yesterday: Mom standing on the landing of the stairs while I sat at the top and watched Dad shout at Mom because she often made mistakes. Dad served in the armed forces, and there was no room for mistakes, especially if he had to repeat himself. This startled me at times, and I would hide under the bed until it was all over. I didn't realize Dad was dealing with the spirit of pride and perfection. He was not even aware of the spirit that was in operation. As a result of all the yelling, Dad allowed an open door for the enemy to plant the seed of fear in my life, which would paralyze me for years to come.

Be aware: Spirits are real and will enter a child's life when he or she is most vulnerable. I encourage all parents to protect their children from the lies of Satan. Yes, it may cost you, but it is well worth it. Start putting an end to Satan's tactics early in the lives of your children. Fight in the Spirit for their souls.

When fighting in the Spirit, we must first be honest and ready to expose Satan, especially when facing real issues including family secrets. Satan's desire is that we keep our issues hidden, bringing guilt and shame and fear in order to prevent the truth from coming to light. The Holy Spirit's desire, however, is to shine a light on those things hidden that we may receive healing and deliverance.

Whenever Mom was pregnant, Dad didn't yell because he was petrified of her losing the baby. When she was expecting her second child, Dad and I were very excited! I would soon have someone to play with. My baby sister was adorable, with the most beautiful hair and eyelashes. It pleased Dad that she resembled him a lot. We were all happy to have her in our lives. As my little sister began crawling and getting into things, I became the go-to person to help her. I can still hear my parents saying, "Grace, go get your sister." My hands were full, and I loved every minute of it.

But when I reached the age of five, things began to change. Dad treated me differently than my little sister, maybe because she was just a baby. It appeared as though he didn't want anything to do with me. I felt that I disgusted him. Whether he realized it or not, I began dealing with a spirit of rejection. Because no one was there to protect me as a child, even more spirits were able to enter. Along with rejection, Satan brought emotional, verbal, mental, and physical abuse. Rejection would be embedded deeply within me, and later in life, I would need much healing and deliverance. In the meantime, I found comfort in food.

The overeating continued. At age six I would sneak extra food after being told no. I got bigger and bigger. Growing up, if your parents said no, it meant no. It would anger Dad, and I received beatings as a result. This all took place while he was home on leave from the service. "It's ridiculous," as he put it. He didn't understand verbal, emotional, and physical abuse just made things worse. I felt horrible about myself. What some may not realize or understand is that feelings of rejection and low self-esteem are the roots, or "the big boys." Roots produce stems and then leaves. I was housing the big boy that would soon produce leaves. I needed God to evict these unwanted spirits from my life. I was so happy when it came time for Dad to return to the service. This would give me a break from all the beatings and abuse.

Shortly after Dad went off to the service, Mom was told she was expecting her third child. We were very happy about our new brother. During this pregnancy, Mom began having complications. While on bed rest, my sister and I cared for her while our dad was away. He was very excited for a son.

At age nine I began cooking and cleaning to help Mom. Since our dad was stationed out of town, my sister and I had to step up. After Mom gave birth to my little brother, she lost a lot of weight. This was a plus for our household since weight was a big deal. Mom wanted to maintain her weight loss, but instead, she began gaining it back. During that time, Dad introduced her to a diet pill to help keep the weight off. Mom eventually became addicted to the diet pills, and much of the responsibility within the house fell to me. When taking the diet pills, Mom was up racing around and cleaning the whole house. But once the pill wore off, she would sleep for days, leaving me to care for my siblings. It was a great responsibility, caring for my siblings.

At age ten, Dad told us that he would be transferred to Cleveland. "I will take the two youngest children, and you take Grace," he told Mom. Mom normally just did what he said, and this time was no different. Dad would arrange for Mom and me to go to Washington and live with his sister until he sent for us. Mom and I were filled with joy to know Dad would send for us.

Dad headed for Cleveland to prepare for my two youngest siblings to join him later. This was the first time Mom and I would be separated from my siblings. On Dad's return, we all met at the airport. It was strange because it felt like we were being ripped apart and would never see each other again. I watched Mom give my brother, who was still in diapers, and my sister over to Dad. They were crying and screaming as we departed the airport. We didn't even get to hug and say our goodbyes the way we wished because Dad was in a rush, saying, "I have to go." I had never seen Mom cry so hard, but she began to comfort me. It was the weirdest feeling. Dad's character was different as he snatched my brother and sister and ran off. Even though we didn't understand what was really happening, I felt in my heart he was not coming back for us. The joy and assurance were all gone.

Two
THE ABANDONMENT

As Mom and I prepared to leave for Washington, we had no idea what we were headed for. Dad's sister lived in a trailer with her boyfriend and a woman, and the couches were seats from an automobile. It was a dysfunctional environment, not fit for a child at all.

Though Mom and I were thankful for a place to lay our heads, something just didn't feel right. And Mom was uncomfortable with me living in a house with a strange man and drug activity. The relationship with my aunt was distant and awkward. It turns out she knew more about Dad than we did.

Three months later and no word from Dad. The allotments had ended. Whenever Mom called the numbers Dad gave her, she was told he wasn't there, and that they would let him know she had called. And every time she called his mom to inquire if she had heard from him, the answer was that she had not. Without the convenience of cell phones, it made it difficult to contact Dad.

Dad's absence and lack of support forced Mom to go to work in order for us to survive and contribute to our stay. She finally landed a job at the mall, but unfortunately, it did not bring in enough income to hire a sitter. Because Mom couldn't afford a sitter, after school I sat on a bench in the middle of the mall, where she could keep a close eye on me while I was thinking and doing my homework. Security guards were so kind to help watch after me as well while Mom worked. When it came time for a break, she brought me treats, doing her best to make sure I was taken care of.

Mom and I had plenty of struggles along the way. I was looking forward to a trip to New Jersey during a break from school. Then one day Mom received a phone call from Dad's mom. "Cindy, I think you need to come home. Matthew sent you a letter, and you need to read it." It was addressed to my grandmother because he didn't want Mom to know his whereabouts. Mom asked if she would read it over the phone, but Grandmother insisted we come home instead.

So we took a train from Washington to New Jersey. The thought that came to my mind was that Dad was telling Mom that he was moving on. I couldn't say it out loud; I was only a child, and I had to stay in my place. When we arrived, I experienced this horrible feeling in the bottom of my stomach. Grandmother met us on the porch with the opened letter, handing it over to Mom. As I sat there, Mom walked to the other end of the porch. After she had finished reading the letter, she began to cry.

I looked at her. "He's not coming back, is he?" I asked. She said for me to be quiet.

Before long, Dad filed for divorce and custody of all three children. He felt he could better provide for us financially and give us a better environment. Mom decided to hire a lawyer and fight back, until Dad threatened her. He threatened that he would inform the court that my grandmother, whom we lived with at the time, sold alcohol out of her home. Mom was afraid and did not want her mom getting into any trouble. She also thought about how everything would go down if she fought, so she decided to allow Dad to have us. When the judge asked whom I wanted to live with, I said my mom. When they asked my sister, she said both. The judge's final decision was to grant Dad full custody of all the children.

Mom was distraught knowing her children would soon be taken away. Seeing that my brother and sister had already lived with Dad from the time he picked them up from the airport, the judge then gave him a day and time to return for me.

I'll never forget the day Dad returned. Mom had

taken me to the back porch of Grandmother's house and began to speak to me about things I needed to know as a woman. I did not understand then, but with time, I was able to figure it out. As we said our goodbyes, tears ran down our cheeks. I could feel my heart beating more rapidly than ever before. I was scared because I had never been apart from Mom, and I did not know what to expect. She hugged me tight and told me she loved me as I went with Dad. I remember looking back and waving as we headed to Cleveland to live my new life.

I could not believe what was happening. It felt like a disaster, and life was about to take a turn for the worse! I went from being a happy, chatty child to one having difficulty concentrating and comprehending homework. It reached the point that I even refrained from communicating. My parents and teachers did not understand how difficult it was for me to concentrate and comprehend. The reason for my difficulties was that I was dealing with grown-up issues.

I just wanted to be a child. Before all the disruptions of rejection and verbal and physical abuse, I received decent grades, Bs and Cs. Sadly, my grades began to drop to Ds and Fs after my parents were no longer together. Dealing with my parents' separation made school even more challenging. I remember being tested by the therapist for learning disabilities. I was asked to build blocks, assemble puzzles, and say words I couldn't pronounce. The therapist my mom took me to while I was living with her was not able to diagnose me properly due to not having enough time. And Mom couldn't help because she was suffering a nervous breakdown due to the trauma in her life, which only God was able to restore.

When someone has experienced trauma, for healing to take place there must be deliverance, which may include counseling. Some may believe counseling is a bad thing, but it has helped me. I am very thankful for the Lord coming to see about me and giving me a mind to seek help. He has allowed healing and deliverance to take place in my life that I may become the person I am today. It is His will that we become the people He intended from the beginning.

Three

ENTERING LIFE
WITHOUT MOM

I'm not ready for this new life, I thought. At the age of ten, Dad and I headed off to Cleveland. It felt like a long ride as I sat in the back seat, looking back. Dad did not talk much, which made for a quiet trip. When we finally arrived, we pulled up to the back of a townhouse. I was shocked to see that he already had a place. I walked inside and found it decorated just as it had been when he and Mom were together, including all the furniture they worked so hard for. It was difficult to see how the house was laid out because of so many family memories. Dad deserted Mom and took almost everything, leaving her with a general relief check of one hundred dollars monthly. I just could not shake the betrayal. I was very hurt! I felt like I had heard too much, knew too much, and seen way too much as a child. This all helped shape the way I viewed my dad. At age ten, most children would be enjoying life, but I was dealing with rejection and hatred.

What others may not realize is that I watched Mom down on her knees crying. And I was there with her, while waiting for Dad's return, living in bad conditions with strangers. I experienced neglect, rejection, rebellion, low self-esteem, unforgiveness, bitterness, hatred, and emotional and mental abuse all because of the way I was treated as a child. I never forgot it, but I had to learn how to forgive!

While scanning over the house, I began feeling very angry. At that point, I knew it was war. While taking it all in, Dad said, "Go upstairs and put your things away. And see your sister and brother." I walked upstairs to where my sister and brother were. To my surprise, two other little girls were there as well, and they kept saying they were my sisters. I absolutely refused to accept it because my father never mentioned them. They were just thrown into my life. It was nothing they did for they were only children.

My dad thought we should agree with whatever. From that moment, I decided, *I am not accepting a new family. There is no way!* I was determined not to adjust to this new life, and I was going to make sure Dad knew it! When my sister said, "Grace, meet our new sisters," I, immediately reacting out of hurt and anger, said, "They are not our sisters!"

Dad had a completely new family. He was determined to erase everything we had known. He went so far as to have someone come to the house to help me with my speech and to learn proper English. I was also taught the proper way to sit and stand, along with how to hold my silverware when eating in a restaurant. He wanted me to be prepared to fit into this new life. But it never happened. I just did not fit into this new life that my dad was trying to push on me. At that time, it just seemed like way too much to take in.

The moment I met Dad's girlfriend, I knew I was going to give her a hard time. As a child, I was just not ready for a new mom that soon. My mom could not be replaced that fast! His girlfriend was very aware Dad was married when she met him; I came across letters she wrote him while he was yet married.

It was too much to take in, and I called Mom and told her what was going on. While Dad and his girlfriend were at work, Mom and Dad's sister made a trip to Cleveland. When they arrived, I let them in the house, not realizing they were carrying a gun. Mom and my aunt went through everything with a fine-tooth comb. Eventually Mom came across a letter addressed to Dad that read, "If you leave your wife and family, I'll give you half of my business." Mom was so upset she called Dad and told him she was at the house and was taking the children. He rushed home, wondering how she was able to locate him. When he arrived, Mom pointed a gun at his face. And before he could react, we left, returning to New Jersey.

Dad came begging for us to come back. I did not want to go. He sat on the floor in front of me, trying to persuade me. Deep down I knew we would have to go back. Dad began threatening Mom that he would take her back to court. She eventually gave in and let him take us back with him. When we returned to Cleveland, I began getting into lots of trouble. I overate and received beatings as a result. As things grew worse, I suffered all types of physical abuse at the hand of my dad. All of which was not normal. I was such a mess that I began stealing food again to fulfill the emptiness in my soul.

I grew up not loving myself. During the Christmas season, Dad would prepare cookie dough and place it in the freezer to be used during Christmastime. I would sneak and pinch from it here and there. By the time Christmas rolled around, the cookie dough was almost gone. This was the worst thing I could have done. Dad went to bake the cookies, and to his surprise, the dough was almost gone. He began yelling and asking if I had eaten the cookie dough. When I replied no, he said, "You better tell the truth." So I said yes. The next thing I remember was a slap and a punch. I hit the floor so hard I thought I was about to pass out. He ran upstairs, took some of my gifts, and threw them down the landing, destroying them. Christmas Day I received a wrapped box filled with empty waxed paper from the cookie dough I had eaten. Dad said he hated me and wanted to kill me.

I realize today my behavior was not acceptable as a child and needed to be addressed, but not in this manner. Thank God that when your mom or dad forsake you, He's always there. Those without positive father figures in their lives may tend to perceive all men as negative. I have made lots of wrong choices due to not having the right perspective of a father in my life. I encourage dads to remain a valuable part of the lives of their children and not allow the devil to get a foothold. I've learned that it's important to know who God says I am and not let others dictate my future. For Thou, oh, God, "hast covered me in my mother's womb, I will praise thee, for I am fearfully and wonderfully made" (Psalm 139:13b–14a KJV).

Knowing the person God says I am allowed me to adjust to my new family. Dad was very busy as a hairstylist and part owner of the salon. He worked from Tuesday through Saturday, sunup till sundown. At times he left me with his girlfriend overnight, and I dreaded it. My oldest soon-to-be stepsister would rape me. She would advise me not to say anything, and of course I didn't tell Dad. He wouldn't have believed me anyway, so what was the use? I was violated night after night until it became normal. As we got older, she apologized, and I forgave her. But I still suffered from the uncomfortable events that eventually resulted in healing and deliverance in my life.

Here we have yet another spirit allowed to enter, lesbianism. What an identity crisis to not know if you like boys or girls. Growing up I always thought I was hiding something.

I began having issues with the way I looked and behaved, which led to seeing a counselor weekly. My

Four

WHAT OTHERS NEVER KNEW

I was introduced to the dean of the boarding school while my stepmom and dad filled out the paperwork. They were given a date and time for me to return, and when I returned, I was there to stay. Dad made certain all records were transferred, which included those involving my behavioral issues and counseling sessions. There was no other way for the school administrator to know my history. As a result, an opinion was formed, and counseling sessions would continue as before. Shortly after enrollment, the students began labeling me as the girl with the issues.

I became close to one of the girls in my cottage. The cottage housed nineteen girls, with up to five to a room, and there was no privacy. It was a set up for the enemy to get a foothold on my life, but today it was a testimony for God's glory. At night, instead of going to sleep, she scooted her bed next to mine and began kissing and feeling on me as she raped me. She told me not to tell anyone. I felt as though nobody liked me, so I kept the secret. I didn't want to lose what I thought was my only friend, so I allowed it to happen night after night. You see, this was normal. There was so much going on in the night, things I was not allowed to talk about.

I needed to feel and know that someone cared despite where I came from. Because I came from an upper-class suburban area, the girls spread rumors that I thought I was better than they, and I talked funny because I spoke proper English. What they didn't understand was that Dad did not allow it any other way, and to do otherwise was not tolerated in our home. I hated this school. Everybody was from the city, and they were rough. If you didn't fit in, you were an outcast, and that was I!

When it came time to return home for holidays and vacations, my parents didn't come for me, like most children's parents did, either because I had gotten in trouble or because my dad was fed up with my mess. I considered this school to be the dreadful school of hard knocks. Once school dismissed for the summer break, off to camp I would go. After arriving, the girls would scramble through my trunk of things Dad had put together. It continued until one day I thought, *Nope, not today, playa.* I put a lock on it. The dorm for boys was located at the opposite end from the girls' dorm. We all came together for dinner and at night for games and movies. Uncomfortable encounters took place as boys were feeling on girls while the staff seemed to pay no attention.

On two occasions while walking to group at camp, I was raped in the woods by a twelfth-grader. I was in seventh grade at the time. I would never say anything because I was so afraid of him. I just put my clothes back on and walked back to the dorm to take a shower. When I arrived, there was a gang of girls prepared to jump me. The boy who raped me told his girlfriend I liked him and he was with me. What a mess this was. After all this, I made up my mind I was going to get kicked out of school so Dad would have to take me to Mom.

That night we had canteen, which was rec. My mind was made up to run away. I ducked and dodged cars and hid. Climbing a tree hoping not to be noticed, I heard barking dogs and the rush of police as they drew closer. I felt sick; I knew it was all over for me. They located me and called Dad to say that they were kicking me out of the boarding school. Just what I wanted.

When Dad arrived to pick me up, he slapped me. "You're going to your mom." *Great,* I thought. When

I got to the house, he packed all my stuff and phoned Mom. "You better take her before I kill her."

Mom answered, "Send her, and I'll be there to receive her." All I can say is, "Thank You, God, for Your rescue, making a way out of no way, and opening doors that no man could shut. Dad placed me on the bus headed to New Jersey once again to live with Mom.

Five

MY NEW BEGINNING

When I reached my destination, I was greeted with a warm smile and a big hug. Mom said, "I don't have much, but what I have you are welcome to." I was just happy knowing I was loved. Stuff didn't really matter.

Life was beginning to look up I thought. Mom enrolled me in middle school, where I completed eighth grade. I graduated and was promoted to high school. But while attending high school, I made bad choices, partying and hanging with the wrong crowd. I began to use alcohol to cover up the things lacking in my life. The drinking got out of hand, which caused me to have blackouts. Mom had no clue as to what was taking place when I left the house. But eventually she somehow became aware and was very upset. She tried encouraging me to stop drinking, but I continued. My everyday routine should have been go to school, get an education, and do my very best. No, not me. I went to school and walked right out the back door to get drunk or high. This continued until one day I was acting silly as always. Mom walked up like, yeah, you're busted. I was scared. I thought my heart was in my shoes. Mom was short in stature but did not play. She never hit me but instead told me where my actions were headed, which gave me a lot to think about. I slowed down for a short while, until I got in with so-called friends, stealing and getting into other kinds of trouble. Because those spirits were not addressed in my life at the time, they just reared back up in a different form. I had to learn that spirits are real and have to be addressed and dealt with. Needless to say, I failed ninth grade because I neglected to attend school and complete my schoolwork. I was ashamed and embarrassed that I had to repeat ninth grade, so I asked Mom if I could transfer to another school and she agreed.

I may have been allowed to attend a different school,

but I made the mistake of bringing along the same issues. I joined other students who would do the dirt along with me. One time my best friend and I went looking for someone to rob. I got so drunk before it all took place. I went over to my grandmother's house to see her before I did my dirt. On the way up in the elevator, this man got off, voicing how he had just received his walking papers and was so happy to be back. I laughed and, being rude, thought, *Oh well, we don't care.* Little did I know God was using him to get my attention. But I couldn't hear because I was so caught up in the way the alcohol had me feeling, drowning out wisdom as it spoke.

As we exited the elevator, my friend and I got on the bus headed downtown. While sitting there looking out the window, we noticed a man walking. He appeared to have money. In our drunken state and not thinking, we jumped off the bus without looking to see that it was filled with witnesses. Our senses were numb. We had no clue and didn't even care. I just wanted it to be over.

After the robbery, my friend and I jumped back on the bus, thinking nothing about it. The bus driver locked the door while yet in park. I thought, *Oh my goodness, we are about to go to jail.* The police entered the bus as my friend and I were ducking and pitching what we had stolen from the man's wallet—five dollars—out the window. We were thrown into a paddy wagon and taken in for booking. Because we were drunk, they allowed us to sleep for a little while.

After waking us up, we were questioned about what had taken place. I told the truth about everything. We were then transported to a juvenile correctional facility, where we spent a month and a half. The judge wanted to try me as an adult because I was seventeen. Thank God that because I had never been in trouble, he had mercy and sent me to a girls' correctional facility instead. We were both sentenced eighteen months. I was devastated and ready at the same time. I said, "Mom, don't waste your money coming to see about me. I did the crime, I will do the time." What I came to understand is that God had His hand on my life, but I was blinded because so many bad things were happening.

My life was in need of a structural change, and if this

was the way, so be it. I thank God for this was truly a learning experience. I do not encourage any young person or anyone else to find yourself in this situation. It will snatch your life away.

I was released on June 10, 1993, the year I would have graduated from high school. When the staff told me, "You will be back," I answered, "Not me. Watch." I meant just that, and I never went back. When Mom arrived to pick me up, she walked right past me, not recognizing me. I had been working out during my stay in the correctional center and lost one hundred pounds.

Little did I know my life was about to change for the better. Mom and I, along with my grandmother, moved from Washington to New Jersey to live with a friend until we were established. Standing and gazing out the window, I began to silently pray, "God, please save me, and I will forgive every person who has ever hurt me. I'm tired. There has to be something better." I began working two jobs until I was able to provide a place of our own. That day finally came, and we moved in. While living in New Jersey, I was missing the guy I had dated while living in Washington. I asked my ex if I could come back, and he said yes. Once my mom and grandmother were established, I was headed back.

After making contact with my ex, we began living together. I was living in sin, and one thing led to another. After a few months of feeling ill, I prayed once again, "Lord, if I'm pregnant, I'll make sure this child will know You all the days of my life. My spirit was crying for a change, but I didn't know how to obtain that." After an appointment with my doctor, it was confirmed that I was pregnant. My boyfriend was happy to hear the news—at first.

He and I had been attending church but had not been converted. One day my sister, her husband, and I were taking a ride. I had received a gift from my daughter's dad that I wanted her to see. It was a brand-new car, right off the showroom floor and customized just for me. You couldn't tell me anything; I thought this was love, but it wasn't. While my sister sat in the car, I noticed something different about her. This wasn't my kicking it partner. She was wearing a skirt, carrying a Bible, and was serious.

Her husband, on the other hand, was sitting in the back seat trying to throw me off, acting like, *Yeah, this is the song right here.* I didn't know God was setting me up. I remember like it was yesterday. I ejected the CD from the car's stereo and thought I was about to jam once I got back into the house.

At home, when I went to insert the CD, my sister stopped me. "Are you ready to accept the Lord into your life?"

I breathed a sigh of relief and replied, "Yes, I'm tired."
She then asked me to lift my hands as she began to pray. I
dropped to the floor and spoke another language for thirty
to forty-five minutes. When I got up, I was a changed
person. My spiritual eyes were open, and I didn't see the
way I had before. I could see spirits and knew things only
God was able to reveal. I was scared at first because all this
was new. I felt complete, like this was what I was missing
my whole life. The feeling was amazing, though, and I
never wanted it to change. I sang and worshipped the best
I knew how. I just wanted to know God on a personal
level. And as I read God's Word, I became enlightened
and convicted of my sins. My sister, her husband, and I
were on fire, witnessing in grocery stores to the point we
called our mom and prayed for her over the phone. She
gave her life to Christ and was instantly filled with the
Holy Spirit that day.

I wanted to remain filled with God's Spirit so I
would not go backward. I asked God to deliver me from
everything I had gotten myself into in order that His will
be done in my life. In reading God's Word, I came across

scripture that spoke of fornicators having their place in the lake of fire. *Oh no,* I thought. I made up my mind to go live with my boyfriend's cousin until we were married.

I was not sure if God was in it. However, one night I overheard my boyfriend on the phone talking with his best friend. "That isn't my baby. She was pregnant when she got here." Even though I was hurt, I immediately forgave to keep my heart free. This being my first child, I showed no reaction, I knew it would be okay. God had another plan, and it was going to work out for my good. I decided to catch the first Greyhound available. I packed, got my ticket, and called my mom, who welcomed me home. I asked if she would prepare a home-cooked meal for the baby and I because I didn't have any extra money; she said yes. I locked the house and left the key. I took the car my boyfriend bought me, and because I was upset, I left it in a no parking zone and placed the club on the steering wheel. Once I stepped onto the bus, I could hear the Lord dealing with me about what had just occurred, and I knew once I reached home, I would have to make it right.

When I arrived in New Jersey, Mom was there to

receive me. She had already cooked, and after eating, I laid down for a nap. I awoke to a phone call from my sister, telling me that my daughter's dad wanted to know where I was and where the car was. I told her she could tell him, and I would call him later. I later called and told him what I overheard. He apologized, and so did I. But the damage had already been done. I wasn't going back into bondage, and this is when my new life with Christ began.

I never imagined I would have to endure the things I went through to become the woman of God I am today. And yes, He's still doing a work in me. I now realize I am a survivor, and God's hedge of protection was upon me with a plan for my life. There were warring and ministering angels encamped about me. The enemy desired that I lose my mind.

I realized that our family had no knowledge of Christ because of Grandmother's rebellion against both Christ and her godly parents. A whole generation was cut off from the knowledge of Christ. My grandmother prevented us from knowing our great-grandmother because she was recognized as a Holy Roller. Thank God for my great-grandmother. She was a praying woman who sent up prayers on behalf of her grands and great-grands. God heard her prayers, and I came to know Christ as a result. Great-Grandmother's prayers were not in vain.

I am very excited to see the next chapter of my life as a child of God. There is so much more to come.

Printed in the United States
by Baker & Taylor Publisher Services